# No Greater Love

### CHARLITA HOUSTON

ISBN 978-1-64140-797-7 (paperback)
ISBN 978-1-64140-798-4 (digital)

Christian Faith Publishing, Inc.
832 Park Avenue
Meadville, PA 16335
www.christianfaithpublishing.com

Printed in the United States of America

To my family, for all their support, and to the one who inspired this book.

# My Reflections/ Author's Notes

It was very hard writing this book. I don't consider myself to be a writer, but I have been known to tell a good story or two. Being that the book focuses on real events, it became hard to decipher what to include in the book and how it should be phrased. God had placed the idea of writing this book years ago, but it wasn't until last summer where I sat down and began. It went through various revisions. My friend, Brittany, who is a professor at Cal State East Bay, read and gave feedback. My daughter, Ottia, made some corrections, and my husband, Sam, gave some fresh ideas on what should be included.

The thing I struggled with the most was whether I should exclude the nurses with as much detail as I did. When they began to encounter life's misfortunates, I started to think that their misfortune was because of them being a part of me and Reed's lives, and for a while, we blamed ourselves. It wasn't until God spoke to me and said that he placed them in our lives strategically. Their need to be complete, delivered, whole, fulfilled, and saved was accomplished by the example Reed and I led. The love we had for each other was so infectious that it drew them to experience true love for themselves. The enemy loves to take credit for what appears to be detrimental, but as the scripture says, "All things work together for the good of them who love God, who are called according to his purpose" (Rms. 8:28), and because these nurses sought after the love of God, they can now see his face in peace.

They all are no longer physically a part of my life, but I still carry each of them with me, and for that I am forever grateful. Nurse Ryan trusted me like no other and taught me to trust in myself. In return, my relationship with God increased and contributed to the woman of God I am today. Nurse Kent kept me on my knees, and he showed me that despite our differences, what we both shared was our love for Reed. Nurse Reggie had my back in many areas in my life. There was a pureness to his love, but even with his challenges, he put every effort into making sure that his love, care, and compassion was shown on a daily basis. Doc was my anchor. He was the one who kept me in place and always helped me recuperate after a battle.

There is so much more I can say about each of them. They trusted me enough to share their families, dreams, fears, and love. Although I was never fortunate enough to see any of them face to face, the relationship we each had was real. I loved them all, and I am so grateful to God that they were a part of my life and that they were integrated in Reed's and my journey together.

# Beginning Quote

We make choices in life. We choose who we will approach and who we will allow to approach us. We decide who we will let into our world and who we will simply dismiss. Some of our choices can be beneficial for us, while others can make us miss out on some of the best experiences in our lives. My perception of one woman almost cost me the experience of a lifetime. My eyes might have deceived me, but my heart led me to uncovering the jewel I had before me. When you take the time to look past what the eye can see, you just might discover something impeccable. I know I did.

# THE MEMORY OF

Imagine the place you feel most at peace. The place where you are the most secured and loved. The place of liberty and unity. Now imagine that this paradise of yours became defiled by the actions of one man. This is what happened to me when I was six years old. My paradise was instantly destroyed. I remember it well. It was a Wednesday night Bible Study. I was in children's church one floor down from the main sanctuary, waiting for the snacks to be passed out. After receiving mine, I walked carefully to the table, avoiding any disturbance that could cause me to spill my drink. I sat down at the end of the table, took a bite of my graham cracker, and as I began to sip my fruit punch, an alarming noise startled me, causing me to spill fruit punch all over the bottom of my dress. I was so afraid of what my mother was going to do when she found out that I didn't even bother to see what caused the noise. Instead, I frantically began looking around for napkins or anything that would clean the mess before anyone noticed. I spotted a pile of napkins from across the room, ran, grabbed them, got on my hands and knees, and started cleaning. Before I could clean up the entire spill, I noticed from the corner of my eye that the teachers were running after the children like a shepherd trying to regain control over their herd. Every child was in disarray, bombarding themselves toward the staircase. I still had no clue what was going on, but I did as all the other kids were doing and figured I'll found out what was happening sooner than later. Looking up from the bottom of the stairs, we saw one of the young adults making his way down. He began yelling, "Pastor just got shot!"

We all started screaming and crying, trying to make our way upstairs but became barricaded by several big-breasted women. More adults started to run downstairs to assist, as children were being peeled off the staircase one by one. The staff began to pass out graham crackers and fruit punch, hoping it would calm us down until our parents arrived. While it only worked for some, the rest of the children were restrained in a small area toward the back of the building until they were calm enough to be released to the rest of the group.

A few hours passed and as we waited for our parents, we could hear the activity of the police officers on the floor above us. With everyone still confused as to who or why anyone would want to kill the pastor, the atmosphere drew still. The cold temperatures of the city had now overtaken the temperature inside, and not a blanket, coat, or heater could bring warmth back into that church.

Earlier that day, the anchor reported that this would be one of Cleveland's coldest nights. The streets became vacant because of the four inches of packed snow, and the only sound that was heard was of the boisterous winds sweeping its way through town. Every business began closing early, except for a few liquor stores and the church, which sat on E181 Street. Compared to anything else around it, the church was a little intimidating at first sight. It stretched for an entire block and had windows as big as billboards. The music that came out of that place could almost put someone into a trance, and despite the freezing temperatures, the parking lot was packed with cars. Someone could easily assume that a celebrity might have pastored the church because of the attention it attracted and the tight security that was seen rotating every fifteen minutes.

Those men who watched the property stood like soldiers and took protecting both the inner and outer realms of the church very seriously. The alpha of the group was a man named Dan. Dan was a six-feet-tall, middle-aged, light-skinned brother who was well-known and respected in the community. Even though he had things handed to him, Dan worked hard for what he wanted. He trained hard to become a police officer for the city of Cleveland. Once he was admitted, Dan served faithfully on the force for ten years, making his way up the ranks. In the prime of his career, devastation came when he got injured on the job, which was followed by the loss of his mother to cancer. Now limited to what he could do, Dan decided to put all his passion into protecting and serving the church. Just as quick as he made rank in his professional career, he accomplished great achievements in the church, making him the head of security. He always made sure the saints were protected and felt safe when he was around.

Upon entering the men's third rotation, they noticed that Dan was missing. They immediately became concerned because Dan was very thorough and accountable in everything he did, so disappearing without anyone knowing where he went was just not like him. Frantically, the men began to look around the parking lot, inside the church, and up the street for any signs of him. Suddenly, one of the deacons spotted Dan's car coming from around the block. He ran toward the car, waving his arms, but was almost hit by a delusional Dan. Once Dan noticed what almost happened, he rolled down the window to see if the deacon was okay. The deacon assured him that he was and asked when he was coming back to the church. Dan explained how he needed some fresh air but will be back before the rotation ended. So the deacon ran back to the church as Dan watched him the entire time through his rearview mirror.

When Dan returned, one of the men asked if he would take over for him inside the church while he walked one of the mothers to their car. Dan was silent and hesitated to move, so the man asked Dan a second time. After taking a long deep breath, Dan agreed and started walking slowly to the side door of the main sanctuary. When he opened the church doors, he was immediately hit with an overwhelming aroma of praise. Everyone was on their feet and the power of God flowed from pew to pew. It became so overwhelming for Dan that he began hiding in every shadow as a way of escape. The more intense the praises, the more disturbed Dan became. There was something obviously wrong with him. While everyone else was on one accord, he was stewing on the sidelines, but even with his weird behavior, everyone was too caught up in the spirit to even notice.

After a while, the praises died down, and the pastor, with his broad shoulders and big round eyes, approached the pulpit and asked the question, "What is love?"

After a few responses, he began breaking down the several types of love and the importance of God's love toward us. By the end of his lesson, the saints had repented hearts, and many began making their way to the altar for prayer. Dan was in the back of the church, pacing back and forth. He was not only upset that his man never returned to his post, but now he found himself being a part of a deliverance service.

Dan waited and waited for the altar to clear up. When it did, he decided that it was his time to make his way down to the altar. As he started walking down the aisle, you could have heard the saints shouting, "Have your way, Lord," "Only you can do it, Jesus," "Deliver, God." When Dan reached the front, he stopped, planted himself firmly, and locked eyes with the pastor. As the pastor began to reach for the oil, Dan reached for his gun and shot the pastor three times in the chest. The pastor fell flat to the floor. Dan then turned around and pointed the gun in the direction of the pastor's wife, but fortunately, she wasn't there, and he was immediately tackled and restrained by the same men who respected and worked alongside of him. The saints were running all over the church in fear, anger, and confusion. Their beloved pastor was gone, and the man they once felt safe around was the very one who took his life. One of the mothers of the church began to implement order, and from that, there was less talking and more consoling. After the police arrived and arrested Dan, he was seen in the back of the police car with a smirk on his face. He shouted out that the enemy told him to kill the pastor, and when he gets out of prison, he was going to come back and finish the job. No one was intimidated by his threats; they were all relieved to see him being put away.

After the police left, the children were released to be with their parents. One of the young adults stayed downstairs with those that were left until it was clear for him to escort them to the parking lot. My mom had already left, so my siblings and I had to wait for one of the sisters of the church to take us home. It was getting late, so those who were left began making their way to the parking lot. The young adult asked if they wanted to see where the pastor got shot. Even though I was scared to, I saw that everyone else was in agreement, and so I just went along. As we came upon the light brown carpet which was now soaked in blood, the tears started to roll. He was not only the pastor of this extraordinary ministry, but he was also my grandfather and my only memory of him was now integrated in this carpet. Stories about him from former members, friends, and family are good to hear, but nothing, nothing would be more imprinted in my memory than the day my grandfather was shot and killed.

# Welcome to Cali

Two years after my grandfather died, my uncle, who was appointed to pastor the church, announced to the congregation that the Lord was sending him to California to start a new ministry. The church members were in shock because they never expected such news and for a ministry they had supported and invested in for years to suddenly end. Some reacted in anger and contested that it was not the will of God, while others honored the decision and some even said they would follow. Despite the reaction of the people, it did not deter my uncle's decision by any means. He knew what he had to do, and so he began the preparations.

Plans were immediately in effect to sell property, belongings, and give the membership time to find a new church home. It wasn't an effortless process however. The stares, accusations, motives all started to surface, but the family knew that anything you try to do for the Lord will have some type of interference from the enemy. With that in mind, we didn't entertain the nonsense; we stayed prayerful and were also excited to be moving to California. Back east, what was seen on television was how we perceived California to be. We would see television shows of stars walking along the beach in beautiful weather year-round, with palm trees as big as the sky, and no cares in the world. We were so happy to be able to get rid of our snow clothes and gear and invest in more shorts and flip-flops.

While we were finishing up selling our property, my grandmother went ahead of the family to get us set up with a place to stay once we got there. The adults in the family were second to go, and by the end of October, those who were left were the grandchildren and my aunt. We took the Greyhound bus and said goodbye to Cleveland as we started on the journey to our new lives which waited for us in California.

After three days on a hot, stuffy bus, we arrived in El Sobrante, California. Our house was in an area where there were lots of fruit trees and plants. I felt as though we were living in a jungle. It was beautiful because I had never seen so much greenery in my life. Our house sat on the top of a hill planted in the midst of green pastures. It was a decent size for a family of six, but with it being fifteen of us, we all had to become creative to make a decent living environment. My grandmother decided to assign one family per bedroom. It was just my luck that my mom had the most kids, five of us to be exact, so you could imagine the space we didn't have. Despite our limited space, my mother expected us to keep it in perfect condition. Everything had a place, and when it was out of place, she would notice. My mom tried to have us honor that concept throughout the house, but with every individual family doing their own thing, it became more of a strain for us all, and so my grandmother made the decision and decided to look for something bigger.

Soon, we moved from El Sobrante to an eight-bedroom house in Oakland down the street from Lake Merritt. By this time, church members from Cleveland started to come, and so we allowed them to move with us until they could get settled and move to a place of their own. The living arrangement this time was that all the adults had their own room, and the families that came down from Cleveland, the female cousins, and the male cousins each shared a room. I didn't mind this arrangement at all. It was better than sharing a room with your mom and brothers. The highlight of staying at this house was that we had a beautiful backyard, a splendid view, and we were so close to the lake that we would go almost every day and perform for the birds and whoever else was watching. Church wasn't that bad either. We had our services in the living room, and for the first time that I could remember, I could go to church wearing pants instead of a skirt or dress.

Following each service, the children would go in the backyard and play while the adults would talk over coffee. I thought we had now entered the good life, but as a kid, my perspective of the good life wasn't the same as the rest of my family. We had differences, and eventually, each household went their separate ways.

However, moving from under one roof didn't stop the family from working together in ministry. We had a storefront church on Foothill Boulevard within a year's time of being in California. Several families joined the ministry and attributed to the start of Prayer Tabernacle. My uncle was young and was still trying to figure out everything that came with pastoring. Although his ways of governing the church were different from my grandfather's, my uncle kept the foundation that was laid, and those from both Cleveland and California respected it and remained loyal to him and the ministry. Besides the church order that my uncle was known for, he exuded an anointing that was like no other. He could preach on a familiar scripture, but it felt as if you heard it for the first time. His revelations were phenomenal, and because of it, people were drawn, which brought an increase in the ministry.

Soon, the ministry began to outgrow the storefront building we were in, so we moved from building to building, trying to find what was compatible for the congregation. We finally settled in a building on San Pablo Avenue. Despite the changes of location, the ministry was flourishing. One Sunday, service was going on as normal, but my uncle wasn't there. This wasn't uncommon because there were many times my grandmother had to start preaching or give words of exhortation before my uncle came. This particular Sunday, my grandmother stalled as much as she could before going ahead and delivering the message herself. After service, the deacons and the administration of the church began looking for him. He was not at home, his friends hadn't seen him, and he told the last person he spoke with that he was leaving but never said where. Later that night, my family got a call by police, saying that my uncle was murdered Saturday night. He was shot in the head and killed while in his car, looking at Christmas lights in the Oakland Hills. Once again, we found ourselves in this familiar situation, and we didn't know what to do. No one was in training to become the next pastor of the church, and we never anticipated another loss. With that, my family was always known to continue in spite of, so the week of my uncle's passing, my grandmother called a church meeting and told the congregation that the ministry will continue because God instructed her to take it over. She asked each person individually if they would support her. Although everyone said yes in that moment, there were some who were really having a tough time accepting having a woman as pastor. After that meeting, some never returned and others eventually faded out, but with those who remained and the leadership of my grandmother, Prayer Tabernacle continued to increase and the vision of those before her continued to be implemented.

# WILL YOU BE MINE

One of the men who stayed and supported the ministry was a young, tall, dark-skinned brother named Sam. He wasn't liked by many of the older members for the reason being that when he came, my uncle immediately took him under his wing and trained him to be the chief administrator, which was a high-ranking position in the church. No one wanted a young man from the streets telling them what to do, however with the passing of my uncle, they no longer had to. His position was immediately stripped from him, leaving him to continue functioning as a minister in which he was called. Despite the changes, Sam remained faithful to Prayer Tabernacle. He was the loyal type and never thought for a minute about leaving because his mentor was no longer with him. He felt that if he was loyal to my uncle and the ministry, then he could be just as loyal to my grandmother. While my uncle was still alive, I noticed him taking an interest in me; however, I was not feeling him at all. Being the square that I was, I found myself attracted to bad boys, but after seeing the company he kept, I had no interest.

After trying to avoid him every chance I had, I noticed something: Sam began to do something other guys in the church didn't. He tried giving me personal attention regardless of my disinterest. A part of me was like "buzz off, homie," while another part of me liked the attention. I started to allow him to come around me, and the more we talked, the longer our conversations got. I didn't know what to think of this. Did he just want some booty, or was he really trying to get to know me? I concluded that he just wanted some booty, and so the part of me that was beginning to feel special quickly dissolved.

One evening, Sam asked my sister to convince me to go out on a double date with him. I looked at her as if she had three eyes on her head. She explained that the other couple will be her and her boyfriend, so there would be no need to worry. After contemplating for a while, I finally told her I would under one condition: she was not allowed to kiss or cuddle on the date. I didn't want Sam getting any ideas. The next night, my sister and I got ready, and as we walked down the stairs, we were greeted by the men holding a bouquet of flowers. He earned brownie points from that, but I needed to see how the rest of the date was going to be before I started giving him any props. When we left the house, we went straight to dinner. After dinner, we took a walk along the pier, gazing at the stars, and for the first time since we've met, I became intrigued. That double date opened the door for more dates, and the more I got to know him, the less walls I built up. Soon I noticed that I was in love, and although I was young and inexperienced with relationships, I knew that this person was going to be a major part of my life.

After one of the church services, my friends and I went in the front of the church near the bus stop, as we did every Sunday. While there, Sam asked if he could talk with me, and before I could answer, he pulled me aside. It appeared to be urgent so I asked what was going on, but as urgent as it seemed to me, he took his time trying to find the words to say. While he was fishing for words, he was also looking down the street. I thought his past caught up with him, and in a few seconds, the police were going to pull around the corner and arrest him. I kept asking him what was wrong as he continued to fish for words. Out of nowhere, the bus pulled up, and as people were getting on, he turned to me and asked, "Will you marry me?" and hopped on the bus. I thought he was going to get off the next stop so I kept looking at the bus, but it just kept going. When I turned around in shock, my little brother was holding a boxed rose and inside was the ring. I just started crying and told the only person I felt would be happy for me and that was my Aunt Candace. Aside from my siblings, I kept it a secret from everyone else. When we would see each other in church, we'll just quickly greet each other and go about our business. When we did announce our engagement, many of the members hadn't known we had been dating for three years. We were young, but we knew how to keep our relationship strong and that was by keeping people out of our business.

May 17, 1997, I became Mrs. Houston. That was a day to remember and the start of my family. After two years into the marriage, we found out that I was pregnant. This was unexpected but a blessing nevertheless. I wasn't sure how I was going to juggle all I had going on and take care of a child. During this time, I was a full-time student, I worked part time, and I was very active in the church. I knew it would be challenging, but since I wasn't doing it alone, I knew I'll be all right.

I was at home one evening, and I just entered my third trimester. Suddenly, I started going into pre-labor. I wasn't too worried because I was told if I didn't see blood then I probably wasn't having a miscarriage, but I also knew that I wasn't supposed to be in labor so I called my doctor anyway. She told me that if I started bleeding to go to the emergency room, but if not, then keep my feet up and rest. As soon as I got off the phone with her, I started to bleed. My husband and I went into the emergency room, and after being there for an hour, no one said anything to us. We asked over and over what was going on, but no one responded. Finally, my husband went out of the room and asked someone at the desk. They explained to us that when we came in, they didn't hear the baby's heartbeat and how they were sorry to have to give us such news. I didn't know what to think. I immediately blamed myself because I figured if I wasn't doing so much stuff, then my baby would be alive. I also began to think of ways I could have prevented this from happening. I had just had my doctor's appointment that Wednesday, I started feeling ill on that Sunday night, and then I went into pre-labor Monday night. I lay there numb, with these thoughts in my mind, while my husband made the various calls to our family. I tried to pretend that I was fine, but I was a complete mess. Soon, they gave me a depo shot, and I began delivering my dead son. When he came out, I looked at him in hopes that he would cry or even move, but the more I hoped, the more life I saw leaving his body. My mom took him away from me, feeling that it would be the best thing to do, and he lay in the bassinet next to me, lifeless. People began visiting and made the experience worse. I had family members tell me that I wasn't strong enough to carry a baby, others told me not to try anymore so I won't and they won't be disappointed again, and the rest took it to church by telling me to re-evaluate my relationship with God. I already lost my firstborn child, and to be told those things really put me into a dark place. I told God if he wanted to take me, it was the perfect time to do so. I felt there was no reason for me to be suffering like that and I just wanted out of here.

After leaving the hospital, the reality was more present. My breast was filling with milk, but there was no baby to sup. I experienced all the pain of childbirth before and after, but there wasn't the privileged of bringing a child home. I had hit an all-time low. My husband and I didn't even talk about it. We were dealing with it in our own separate ways, but despite how broken I was, I knew that staying home was not going to make it better so I continued going to church as normal. One Sunday, I asked God to take all the hurt away. I was tired of asking questions and blaming myself, and I just wanted to get on with my life. God's response came quickly through a positive pregnancy test just a few months after having my son. I looked up to heaven and was like really God. I told myself that maybe God had given me a second chance, and for that, this time, I was going to do things differently. For one, I stopped working and just concentrated on school, and the auxiliaries I was a part of in church became minimal. I was told that the schedule I had before was not the cause of my stillborn; however, I didn't want to take any chances. I also kept this pregnancy a secret. I didn't completely trust that God would allow me to have a healthy baby, and in the case that I have another stillborn, I wouldn't have the shame I had before.

As the baby began to grow, I waited for any familiar signs I had with my son, but remarkably, none came. Two weeks before the due date, the baby decided to come early, and I delivered my beautiful baby girl. When I heard her cry, my heart filled with joy. I realized that I was strong enough to carry and deliver a child and that it was worth trying again. Despite my naysayers and the fact that I doubted God, he still blessed me. I asked God why he would allow me to have my daughter after I doubted him. He told me, "Because under that doubt, was a mustard seed of faith and as the baby began to grow, so did your faith. It not only produced one child but three children, my family," and as I processed the words that was given from God, I thought about how one double date started my forever.

# The Escape

From the experience I had, some would think that my relationship with God would began to fade; however, it became stronger. I began studying the word more and became more active in church. During this time, the church was very busy. We had just entered into a new organization, which made us the hosting church for the fellowship meetings in our area. These meetings gave us the opportunity to meet likeminded people. One clergy woman I came across was a woman by the named of Cynthia Reed. She had an incredible story of what she went through as a child, and it all started fourteen years before I was born.

"You're just like your daddy," rang in the ears of Reed day in and day out. Being very young, she had little to no memory of her father. All that was given to her was the toxic description that rolled from her mother's lips. The older she became, the more she resembled her father, which made her mother resent her more. With this type of treatment she encountered daily, it became Reed's norm. She knew it wasn't the greatest thing but it was familiar, and that was something she felt she could live with. Soon, Reed discovered that her normal life would be interrupted when her mother announced that there will be an addition to the family; she was inheriting a stepfather and stepbrother. Reed thought with this new edition, things would get better; she could finally have the family, but the minute they moved in, she discovered that her new family would only be an addition to her pain.

One Tuesday afternoon, Reed came home from school and went straight into the kitchen to get some food from the refrigerator. When she pulled the handle, it wouldn't open. She looked down and saw that there was a lock on the refrigerator door. Feeling confused, she ran into the living room and asked her mother about the lock on the refrigerator door. Her mother responded, "I put it there so you won't eat us out of house and home. From now on, you are restricted on what you can eat."

Reed was dumbfounded; she had no clue where this was coming from. Did the stress of having more people in the home become too overwhelming for her mom, she wondered, or was this just some type of temporary punishment. Well, whatever the case, Reed always did what her mother said, so she went back into her bedroom hungry.

As the weeks and months rolled by, Reed found herself eating less and less. While the family sat down for dinner, she would sit in the living room, on top of a big fluffy white rug, waiting for them to finish eating. Once they were done, she would go in the kitchen to get whatever scraps were left. After a while, she noticed that less food was being left on the plate, so she became clever and started to store food away while either preparing it or cleaning the kitchen after dinner. It worked out for a while until her mom caught on to what she was doing and banned her from the kitchen altogether. That was a setback for Reed. She had no money and no other means of getting food. It had gotten to a point where her stepbrother felt so sorry for her that he would throw apple Jolly Ranchers at her from time to time. It was appreciated, but it wasn't enough to keep a starving girl satisfied, so Reed developed a plan.

One morning, Reed woke up, eager to get to school. She jumped out of bed, washed her face, brushed her teeth, got dressed, and headed to school earlier than normal. Reed knew the routine of how each child would put their lunches in a big red bin before entering the classroom. This particular day, Reed eyeballed each child who dropped their lunches in the bin and made a mental note of whose lunch she was going to take while everyone was at recess. When recess approached, Reed hid in the coat rack until she saw that the room was cleared. She peeked around the corner and immediately snatched two lunches and hid them in her jacket as ran out. When lunch came, she found a secluded area and began to devour those lunches (as if she was a bear coming out of hibernation) before heading back to class. Her strategy seemed to work for a while until the teacher was approached by numerous children with missing lunches, so the teacher decided to lock the lunches in her desk, and Reed no longer had access to them. That didn't stop her, however, from continuing to think of clever ways of getting food, but with every failed attempt, her mother was notified, and Reed was punished by being locked for hours in a dark closet with the family cat. This experience became so traumatic that her quest for food ended.

One early morning, Reed found herself unable to sleep. She was contemplating whether she should run away or continue to stay and be treated as she was. She looked at the clock; it was 5:00 a.m. Her leaving would be the only way she would survive, and so while everyone was sleeping, Reed snuck quietly into the kitchen, looking in the couch cushions for loose change. When she couldn't find any, she went into the kitchen and took some change her mother kept in the cookie jar, got a few snacks, and left out the front door. Reed was very familiar with the bus line because she had to catch the bus to school, so she waited for the bus and stayed on until its last stop, which was the train station. She then decided to catch the train to Los Angeles. When Reed arrived in Los Angeles, with nothing left in her pockets, she just sat on the bench, hungry, clueless, and alone. After ten minutes of Reed being there, she was approached by a tall black male, who wore a brown hat and a long trench coat. He asked Reed was she lost. She responded by saying no. He then asked her if she had any place to go. Reed looked up and slowly shook her head. He asked one last question and that was did she want to go with him. Being only fourteen years old, Reed knew right from wrong, but she felt that nothing would be worse than what she'd just escaped from so she took his hand, looked up, and said, "Yes, yes, I do."

# The Change

After leaving the train station, the tall young man drove them to his apartment, which overlooked the city. When they entered, he took off his hat, his long trench coat, and placed them neatly on the coat rack. He sat Reed down and gave her the house rules. One rule he made prominent was that she had to address him as guardian. Although Reed was feeling uneasy with the decision she made, a small part of her felt a security in which she hadn't felt in a while.

As the days progressed, Reed watched how different people interacted with her guardian. The admiration, respect, and fear seemed to coexist within them all. Reed began to become more curious of this man she now called guardian, and the uneasiness of the entire situation soon faded away.

One night, Reed asked why people responded to him the way they did. He told her it's because of his position. He was the captain of a gang in a certain area, and everything in that area was orchestrated through him. He saw her curiosity and asked if she wanted to learn the business. Being only fourteen and having a sense of independence, Reed responded without hesitation and said yes. Her guardian explained how he was going to spoon-feed her his life lessons, and he started by picking up a broom. He began sweeping the floor and told her pay close attention because what was being shown was expected from her when she had to do it. For the next few days, Reed imitated everything her guardian showed her, and for the first time, she was starting to feel wanted because of the attention and the ongoing compliments given by her guardian. Reed started to feel more at home, and the void she once had was now filled with a sense of family.

One evening, Reed was told by the guardian that for her to be considered a part of the family, he had to beat her into it. Fear rose in Reed to the point that she became as stiff as a board. From what was implied around the house, she knew this day would come and knowing the process didn't make it any better, but Reed thought of how she never felt a part of anything before being with the guardian, so she looked up at him and he took her hand and led her outside. Once outside, they got into a car and drove to a remote location. When they arrived, Reed stepped out and was immediately hit on the side of the head. She went down as more blows were added. By the end of the beating, the family stood her up, and they all rejoiced, welcoming her as one of them. At that point, Reed no longer thought about the pain but more of the celebration. This was a celebration for her, and now she had a family, a family that made her feel as though she belonged.

Soon, Reed began to have a routine of her own. She would go to school during the day and gangbanging at night. She never understood why she was made to go to school while the other girls were working during the day. Her guardian expressed to Reed that he wanted her to finish her education and didn't want to rob her of having somewhat of a normal life. He expected Reed to bring home good grades as well as handle her business on the streets at night. To help her accomplish that, the guardian began to cut back on some of her responsibilities both in and out of the house. Out of everyone, Reed was the only one who stayed with the guardian. She was made privy to things others had no clue about, and a sense of trust became the dominant connection between Reed and her guardian. She knew not to repeat anything that was done or said in the home, and the guardian knew she could be trusted.

One night during one of her runs, Reed was told to deliver a package to two black males waiting at Jefferson Park. Being bored, Reed decided to have a little fun. When she approached the men, they handed her the money and she took off running. She hopped a fence, they hopped a fence, she rolled over cars, they rolled over cars, whatever she did, they did, and they were gaining on her. After exhausting places to turn to for escape, Reed saw a church who apparently was having service from what she could tell, so she ran in. When she went through the doors, Reed headed straight to the front, making her way to an empty pew. It was amazing to know that the pew she chose was the only one that wasn't packed with people, and because there were so many people everywhere else, the men had no clue where Reed went. They then decided to go up to the balcony to get a better view, but when they did, they still were unable to spot her and so they left. Not knowing that they left, Reed continued to hide under the pew, when suddenly, she heard the preacher say, "If you want to be baptized, go to the back with Sis. Willis."

Reed thought this would be her chance to escape before finding her, so she ran into the arms of Sis. Willis looking back for the men the entire time. When they got to the back, Sis. Willis asked if she knew what it meant to be baptized. Still on guard, Reed quickly answered no, and Sis. Willis sat her down and began to explain the baptism and receiving of the Holy Ghost. By the time Sis. Willis was finished, Reed was pricked in her heart, and she turned over the money, drugs, and gun to the deacons. They led Reed to be water baptized in Jesus's Name and then brought her to the upper room to tarry with her until she received the Holy Ghost.

Before leaving, Reed had to process what just happened to her. She knew her life had changed in one night because she felt different, looked different, and no longer had some of the desires she had before. Reed felt a freedom that was much different than being with the guardian. It was as if the limits were taken off, and there was nothing she wasn't capable of doing. Although she was ecstatic of her new life, she knew her guardian wouldn't be as happy. Reed began to fear the worst. She knew the consequences of her returning with no money and no drugs but instead with a story he wouldn't comprehend. In fear for her life, Reed decided not to return home. During the day, she would roam the streets when she wasn't at church. At night, when the church services were over, Reed slept under cargo trucks as they parked at rest stops. With this new routine, she understood that it would be a matter of time before she was paid a visit by her "family." She then decided to go to her guardian before he came to her. Reed knew that her only option of leaving the family was through death, but with God now in her life, she figured she had nothing to lose. Knowing her guardian's routine, Reed waited until she knew he would be home alone. As she was walking up the stairs, she began rehearsing everything she was going to say. She knocked on the door, and when he opened it, neither of them said a word, as Reed started to walk toward the couch. Her guardian calmly asked, "Where have you been?"

Reed immediately went to the point of how she was chased by men, so she ran into a church to hide but ended up being baptized and receiving the Holy Ghost and was a changed woman. After she was done, the guardian told her that she must choose between the family or dying for her newfound faith. Reed pleaded for him not to take her life and promised that everything she ever saw, heard, or was told while being there would stay with her until the day she died. The guardian took her by the shoulders and threw her into her bedroom. Paralyzed with fear, Reed didn't move a muscle the entire night. The only movement that was made was from the guardian pacing back and forth throughout the night.

The next morning, while Reed was still subjected to her room, she heard her guardian approach the door. He walked in, gave her a plate of food, and slammed the door shut without saying a word. Reed felt so bad and couldn't stop blaming herself for putting her guardian in this predicament. She knew that he still cared for her or she wouldn't be in his apartment with a plate of food before her. All she could do now was wait.

Night came, and the guardian told her to come out the room. He told her that he will allow her to live under one condition, she had to be beaten out of the family, and if he heard that she said anything to anybody, he would find her himself and kill her. Reed couldn't thank him enough because she knew this was a rare exception. She immediately took the consequences, and before leaving, Reed thanked her guardian for what he taught her, the love that was given, and most of all, for sparing her life. Reed walked away from there, bruised but not broken; she was free and in the position to now accept help from church members without their lives being in danger. Although Reed often reminisced of how it was living with her guardian, she never regretted her choice to leave. Her relationship with God became priority, and it was all because of one act of boredom.

# My First, My Last, My Everything

The church became Reed's second home. She was found there for noonday prayer, evening service, choir rehearsal, minister training, and everything else in between. On the Sunday of January 1982, the church was entering a revival. Revivals usually last from a few days to a week, packed with great speakers, good music, and great fellowship. A part of fellowship was going out to eat afterward, and this was something that Reed and her crew did often. On this night, instead of them going out and being among themselves, they decided to join another young group of people. When they arrived at the restaurant, Reed's crew sat her next to a young man named James. He was one of the choir directors at the church as well as a national evangelist, which required him to do a lot of traveling. Reed would see him from time to time but never took notice to him. She figured this time since they were sitting next to each other, she could at least get to know a little bit about him. They began by asking questions and talking about their common interest in church. As the conversation developed, the more comfortable they became. At the end of the meal, they found themselves completely indulged but knew it was time to say good night and so they did and went their separate ways.

Three days later while in service, James sent a note to Reed, asking her if she would go out to eat with him and a few other people after service. She agreed and soon found that this was something that became a regular thing. Eight months into the relationship, they were officially a couple. Everyone was ecstatic with the idea of them being together, except for the few haters who wanted James for themselves. When James was approached, he would politely let the women know he was not interested and bragged so much about Reed that it repelled them from coming around. Reed and James made it even worse for anyone who hated on their relationship by dressing alike. Every service, they were found wearing the same colors, and if they didn't have it prior, James would go out and buy whatever was needed. It went from dressing alike to James teaching Reed what it was to have a gentleman in her life. He would open and close doors for her, walk on the outside of the sidewalk, pay for her meals, wait for her after church services to assure she got home safely, and to put the cherry on the cake, he would even have her bath water ran before she got home. From the moment they started their relationship, they had a tradition that no matter if James was in the field or at home, they were to talk during the same time, every day. James never missed a phone call, and Reed expected nothing less.

It was thirteen months into the relationship and everything seemed to be going well. On this Sunday before the dismissal, the Bishop asked Reed if she would approach the pulpit. After being nudged by one of her friends because she wasn't paying attention, Reed slowly approached the pulpit and ended up next to James. The Bishop looked at James and said, "He got something he wants to say to you."

As James approached Reed, the choir of one-hundred-plus voices stood up. James started to openly reminisce of their relationship. He stated how he knew she was going to be his wife the first time he laid eyes on her at the restaurant, and although she makes him upset from time to time, some of his happiest moments was knowing that at the end of the day, he would be able to talk with her. James ended by kneeling and saying, "Will you be my partner for life? Will you be my wife?"

Reed was frozen. She didn't know what to say, so the Bishop came and helped her by whispering in her ear, "This is the time for you to say yes."

Reed said yes, and James took off running around the entire church. The congregation went up in praise, and the choir, who was supposed to be singing during this time, were all a wreck. After circling the building, James went back to help Reed to her seat, but when they got close, they started shouting together and the celebration continued.

Three days after the engagement, James had to leave on assignment. They continued their daily routine of phone calls, but the focus was now on the preparation for the wedding. James was the one who did most of the planning while Reed was the one to implement them since he was away a lot. During this time of preparation, James was offered to pastor a church in Idaho. Reed was of no interest but told him to ask as many questions necessary before deciding. On the last night of James being in Idaho, he decided that he was going to take the position, but he let them know it would be after he got married. They agreed, and from that point on, it seemed that things were really picking up for him and there were national churches now asking for him to come and minister. James became so busy that a week and a half before the wedding, he flew down to do a quick dress rehearsal before getting on a plane to New York.

Reed knew that after James arrived in New York, he was going straight to the church to preach and then head to the hotel for their nightly conversation. She sat by the phone, but at the usual time he would call, he didn't. Reed started to worry, knowing that this wasn't like him; he never missed a call. She tried calling the hotel he was staying at, but they told her that he hadn't arrived yet. Thinking how strange it was, Reed decided to call a few of his friends to see if they heard anything from him. They told her no but not to worry. Reed reluctantly waited as she fell asleep on the couch holding the phone.

The next day, Reed woke up early and decided to run to the grocery store before heading back home to be planted next to the phone. On her way there, she saw her friends, Mel and DJ, outside of Mel's house. She thought it was strange because DJ lived nowhere around them, and for them to be outside that early in the morning was odd. However, Reed continued to go to the grocery store. When she came back, they were still outside, and this time, she stopped.

She asked them what was going on and told them how she hadn't heard from James. Suddenly, Mel jumped on Reed's back, trying to restrain her while yelling for DJ to tell her. DJ said that James's dad called her last night and told her that James was in a car accident and was immediately killed. Reed gave no response. She went in her car, drove home, called his dad to make sure it was true, and stayed in her apartment without saying a word. Her friends always had keys to her apartment, so every day, there was someone always there to be with her, but Reed remained disconnected from the world.

A month later, the church was doing a fund-raiser, and they had the Clark sisters as their special guest. One of Reed's friends bought her a ticket and to make sure she went her friend went to Reed's apartment, helped her get dressed, and drove her to the concert. Still being disconnected from the world, Reed just sat there as the concert went on. During the last songs from the Clark sisters, there was a loud screeching sound that surfaced from Reed. She continued screaming to the point that everyone cleared the sanctuary, except for Reed's friends. They were there for hours, but because of Reed's friend, Stephanie, talking her through the process, Reed eventually got delivered. Now that she was back into reality, she had to go through the process one would when losing a loved one. It wasn't easy, but since Reed had those who were still coming around and being very supportive, it made the grieving process that much easier to handle.

# Our First Meeting

After two years since the death of her fiancé, Reed decided to move back to San Diego to start anew. She continued to be as passionate about ministry as she was in Los Angeles and was soon to become a traveling evangelist, like James. On this Sunday, it was considered one of the hottest weekends of the year, and my church service ended earlier than normal in preparation for the evening service. I was scheduled to nurse that night, and as a nurse, my responsibilities were to attend to the needs of the pastor as well as any visiting pastors. When I was not called on, I would stand in front of the big blue door to prevent anyone from bothering the pastor.

When the evening service approached, I ran into the sanctuary in fear that I was late, put away my belongings, fixed my nurse hat, which seemed to be always crooked on my head, and ran to my post. After letting the pastor know I was there, I instantly scoped the main sanctuary. Everything seem to be in order, except for this figure all the way in the back of the church. It was hard to see who or what it was because it blended in with the building's shadows, and since I thought everyone had cleared the sanctuary, there was no way I was going to take a second look. Suddenly, I heard a crack from the big blue door, and the pastor peeked out and asked me to approach the figure in the back of the church and asked if they wanted anything to eat. I immediately said yes ma'am and started toward the back. Although I now knew the figure wasn't something supernatural, I still felt sweat buds starting to form between my thighs. I paused and took a deep breath as I proceeded down the aisle, which in my mind had turned into death row. You would have thought an electric chair waited for me because the closer I got, the heavier my sweat became and the more unpleasant I began to feel. When I got to the back, I noticed that the figure was a woman. A woman with a firm stature and a demeanor that read, "If you come close to me, I'll cut you." Her arms were folded across her chest, and her uninterested eyes scanned me up and down. Fearful of what her response would be, I slowly asked, "Would you care for something to eat?"

She immediately said, "No thank you," in a tone of dismissal, so I took her tone as a sign of relief and gladly returned to the big blue door to give my report.

Soon, people started to pour in, and it was time for service to start. During praise and worship, the praises of the people were so high that everyone was on their feet. As I began worshipping God with my eyes closed and my hands lifted, I heard through the microphone, "And while the presence of the Lord is here, we are going to have Evangelist Cynthia Reed from San Diego to minister to us this evening."

I opened my eyes and saw the woman who was in the back of the church with the firm stature and threatening demeanor approach the front. My first thought was to get as far away from her as possible. I did not want to be on the frontline as she put the fear of God into the people. But then I thought, *Wait a minute. I can't go anywhere. I am still on duty, which means I must stay close to Pastor.* So I just stood there, uneasy. Three minutes had passed since Evangelist Reed went up and she still hadn't said a word. After she saw the people coming down from their high praise, she grabbed the microphone and said, "Let's give the Lord a handclap praise."

That little phrase had the people instantly hooked, and the more she began to talk, the more impressed I as well as the people became. I couldn't understand how this scary, intimidating woman from earlier could be so powerful and mesmerizing. The words that she spoke were like honey, thick, rich, and hard to remove. She had a flow to her that made it hard to believe there was nothing more than a Bible to assist her, and the more we heard, the more we became addicted.

Toward the end of her message, Evangelist Reed dropped a bombshell. She told the people that she had been battling with stage 4 pancreatic cancer ever since her late twenties. She went on to say that despite the illness and childhood experiences, God has allowed her to continue living. When doctors, nurses, and even close friends gave up on her and told her there was nothing more they could do, God never gave up on her. His undying love is what kept her here thus far, and for the rest of her life, she will tell of his goodness. After Evangelist Reed's testimony, there wasn't a dry eye in the building. How could someone who constantly had to endure so much pain still has a desire to work for God as hard as she did. I felt so bad. My judgment about her was totally off and I knew I had to make it right, so I decided that after church I was going to go to her and apologize.

Service ended around midnight, and when I looked to find Evangelist Reed, she had a line of people waiting to talk with her. I still had some more things I needed to do before I could be relieved so that would buy me some time to allow the line to die down. As I continued to finish my duties, I noticed the line getting shorter. Soon, she was on the last person, and before I could get to her, she had been escorted by the deacons to her car. I was so mad. I just knew that I blew my chances of apologizing and wasn't sure if or when I would see her again. I finished up what I had to do and began walking to my car in great disappointment. While crossing the street, I was suddenly cut off by a white jeep. When I looked into the jeep, I saw Evangelist Reed on the passenger side, signaling for me to come. I ran to the side of the door, and before I could get a word out, she looked at me, gave me a smirk, and said, "Here's my number, call me any time," then they drove off. I looked at the number and smiled.

# GETTING TO KNOW YOU

Three years had passed since the first night Reed and I met. I had three kids by that time and was preparing to move back to California after living in Virginia for about a year. As I was packing, I noticed a small piece of paper in one of the purses I barely wore. Instead of throwing it away as I normally would have done, I unfolded it and noticed that it was Reed's phone number. I couldn't believe I still had it after all this time. As I was about to throw the paper away, assuming her number was no longer valid, my better judgment wouldn't let me. I just put the number somewhere I knew I wouldn't forget and told myself that I would call as soon as I returned to California.

A few months went by and my family and I were now in California staying with my oldest sister. My sister began telling me of all the great church services I'd missed and how wonderful it was when Reed came down to do a revival. Since Reed joined the same organization that my mom and the church was a part of, she became close friends to both my mom and my eldest sister. After finding out the connection she had with them, I wasn't sure if I wanted to have any personal connection of my own. When it came to being involved with my family, we either had those who were not able to separate individual relationships or a family member who became possessive over that common friend. Either way, it always ended up messy, so to avoid it altogether, I decided I would not call.

A few weeks into my return, I was feeling lost. I was lost mentally, emotionally, and spiritually. Every time I wanted to talk to someone, Reed would pop up in my head. I tried to dismiss the thought and looked to see if I had other options, but sadly, I didn't. One night, I decided that I'll call her. I figured she might not have the same number anyway, which made my attempt that much easier. When I dialed the number, the phone rang, and to my surprise, Reed picked up. Shocked as I was, I started the conversation by introducing myself, but soon realized there was no need for an introduction because she knew who I was right away. Once that was established, I began talking on generic topics just to feel her out. I guess throughout the conversation, she was giving good vibes because the next thing I knew, I started to unleash everything I was feeling. Things that I held in for years began to spill out. I felt so liberated, and the thing about it was that I didn't care about her relationships with my family, nor the fact that I barely knew her, all that mattered was that I felt comfortable. We spoke for hours, and it felt as if we had always been a part of each other's lives. The more we talked, the more intrigued I became and I was eager to develop this new friendship. After that one conversations, our communication went from once a week to every other day, and what was so great about it was that I always left a conversation with some type of revelation of either God's word, life in general, or on my personal circumstances. I started to look to Reed as a mentor; she had an answer for everything and what she advised would always be what I needed.

One night, while we were having one of our daily conversations, Reed said that she and my mom were talking and she decided that she was going to move from San Diego to Oakland to help my mom in ministry. After hearing that, I couldn't have been happier. My friend was going to be living closer to me and attending the same church. I responded by asking her if there was anything I could do, but to my surprise, she already began the process, so it wouldn't be long before she came.

Several weeks had passed, and Reed arrived a day early. I knew I would see her that night at church and I couldn't wait. We talked on the phone that day until it was time for us to leave for service, and once I arrived, Reed was already there sitting in the back of the church, waiting to speak with my mom. I went to her and we embraced. Before I could get two words out, my mom called her into the office. For the rest of the night, Reed became like a passing ghost. This was not what I expected when seeing her for the first time as my friend, but I understood the politics of church well and what you must do might supersede what you want to do, so I just kept my feelings intact and enjoyed the service. The service ended around 11:00 p.m., and as I was saying my goodbyes, Reed had someone to tell me not to leave before seeing her. My first reaction was "Oh, now you have time for me," but I quickly got over my feelings and went to see what she wanted. When I sat down, she gave me this big smile and embraced me as if I was a long-lost cousin. There was nothing I could do but smile. We started talking and laughing until we noticed that almost everyone had cleared the church, and we were about two seconds from getting kicked out ourselves. I walked her to her car, told her to be safe, and sent her on her way.

One Sunday afternoon, my mom called Reed into her office. After being in there for a few hours, Reed left the office looking confused and very upset. I followed her and asked what happened. She didn't say a word, didn't even look at me. She just walked straight out the front door. That night, I tried calling her and every day since, but there was no response. A part of me knew that this was going to happen eventually because of her involvement with my family, but another part of me felt that our bond was so strong that she wouldn't just leave without saying anything to me, so I decided to give her some time to cool off before attempting to reach her again.

That following Sunday, Reed didn't show up to church. She never missed services, so I knew what happened was more serious than I thought. At the end of service, my mom, the pastor, announced to the congregation that Reed was no longer a part of the ministry. My heart broke instantly because she left without saying anything to me, and I thought that was something she would never do. She cut all ties, and once again, I found myself suffering from the actions of my family. For days, I went into a phase of beating myself up for getting so close to a person that were also friends with my family. There were many nights where my husband just held me and let me cry and vent. I was tired of being disappointed by those closest to me, so for the most part, I pretty much stayed to myself

One night while in bed, God talked to me and told me that I finally saw the human side of Reed. For so long, I was looking at her as this supernatural being and never really took notice to the human side of her. She could be lost and confused just like anyone else, and whatever was done or told to her in the office that night hurt her deeply. Reed have always had a history of people hurting her, so when she gets hurt, she completely shuts down and detaches herself from everyone. With me knowing this, through my own hurt, I became more passionate for hers.

A few years had passed since Reed left, we were invited to fellowship with a church whose pastor was a former deacon of ours. When we walked in, I saw the back of Reed and was stunned to see her there. She had now become a part of his ministry, working as the pastor's aide. Seeing her there made me very uncomfortable. Throughout the service, I did everything I could to avoid her. I made it to the end of the service without having to say a word, and now it was time to leave. As my husband and I were walking out the door, we were told that the pastor wanted to have words with my husband. I was so mad, but there was nothing I could do, so I sat in the sanctuary watching everyone else leave. I looked up and in comes Reed. She sat down on the opposite side of the pew without saying a word. I didn't know what to say or if I even wanted to say anything to her, so we just both sat there in silence. After noticing that my husband and the pastor was going to be awhile, Reed began to spark up a conversation. We started by talking about what was going on in our lives and the crazy stuff we had been experiencing, but not once did either of us bring up the past. The more we talked, the more comfortable we became, and it started to feel like old times. Just as we were getting familiar with each other, my husband came out of the pastor's office and asked if I was ready to go. I look at Reed, she looked at me, and we just embraced each other. I then walked out the door and headed toward my car. Before I could get far enough, I heard Reed call my name. I turned and ran back, then I asked her was there something I forgot. She looked at me and said, "Yeah, you did," and then she handed me a folded piece of paper with her number on it. We both laughed as I took her number, and I told her, "I'll give you a call sometime."

# THE BATTLES BEGIN

After leaving my mom's church, Reed moved to various locations before finally settling in Sacramento. Prior to her settling down, we would only talk while she was working the graveyard shift because our schedules changed. Plus, she would say when she talked with me, it would help her to get through the night. I was starting to become very concerned for her however. Not only because she was working late at night as a gatekeeper, but her battle with cancer was becoming more difficult. The more difficult it became for her, the more things I dropped from my daily life to make sure I was available whenever needed. At first, it was challenging to be there for Reed as I desired since people came in and out of her life. Reed wasn't sure if she wanted me to know so much about her illness, but after a while, it didn't matter because the illness spoke for itself. From that point on, I told Reed that we were in this together, and no matter what type of information she received, God would always have the final say so.

For many days and nights, I found myself on the phone helping Reed get through the pain. Sometimes, she would even go in and out of consciousness, between life and death, and I would have to pray her back to life. This happened more than I could count. It was something I felt was beyond what I could do, but I knew I couldn't let Reed down nor could I let God down who had charged me as protector of her life. She wasn't ready to die and I wasn't ready to let her go, so when I prayed on her behalf, I would always ask for guidance, strength, and faith and God would always answer.

After a while, Reed began to inherit other ailments. She started having multiple seizures and soon developed a brain tumor, which caused constant migraines. At this point, the pain medicine she received from the doctors were like baby aspirin because her body had become immune to it. I didn't know what to do. It would be weeks before she would have somewhat of a decent night's sleep, and it would always break my heart to hear her suffer like that, so I prayed and asked God for guidance.

One night while we were talking, the idea of hospice came to mind. I explained to her that with hospice, she would be checked on every day, and they would also provide services to assist her with everyday activities. Reed thought it was a clever idea but told me she was already on hospice a year before we met and they kicked her off because she didn't die within the allotted time they give their patients. I told her that we should try again because it's a year later and it would make me feel more at ease since I lived seventy-six miles away and wouldn't be able to get to her immediately if needed. She agreed and we began making the arrangements.

A few weeks went by and Reed was set in hospice. Although the hospital policy stated how their employees were not allowed to share any information with anyone outside of the patient's family, I felt relieved and I knew that this was the best thing for both Reed and I. Getting into the program was the easy part, now it was time to find her a nurse. Reed was prejudiced when it came to certain types of nurses because of past experiences, so we had to make sure she would find one she was comfortable with. After an intense search, Reed selected a man named Nurse Ryan. Nurse Ryan was tall, muscular, and wore a long ponytail. He grew up in a single-parent household, which made him become a man at a very early age. When he learned that his mother had cancer, he began to care for her up until the time she passed (which he was sixteen at the time). From that point on, he moved in with his aunt, graduated from high school early, and enlisted in the marines for four years. While in the marines, Nurse Ryan went to school for oncology, but after he received his degree, he felt he wanted to give people the dignity and care they deserve during their last days so he transferred to the hospice division.

When Nurse Ryan arrived, you could tell right away that he was very professional. His reports were always thorough and detailed, and before he left from Reed, he would always go over what he had discovered during her physicals, and knowing the relationship she and I had, he would insist for her to give me the updates as well. His visits became more frequent and his time spent became longer. The more Nurse Ryan began to tend to Reed, the more personable he became with her. He started going above his duties and responsibilities by doing things like running her bath water, straightening her room, and sometimes, cooking for her the only thing he knew how, eggs. Nurse Ryan got so attached that he decided if need be, he would go against policy to contact me. He knew that I looked after Reed and was the most prominent person in her life, so when there were times I didn't hear from Reed because she was either in the hospital or in so much pain, he would inform me by either texting me from Reed's phone or from his work cell phone, so if questioned, he could say that he never talked with me directly.

With the time Nurse Ryan, Reed, and I spent together, we were becoming like the three musketeers. He gave me information on Reed's condition, I asked questions if needed, and we both did everything we could to care for Reed. Nurse Ryan not only dealt with natural things, but he was beginning to witness spiritual battle between Reed, myself, and the enemy. It wasn't until then when he began to ask me personal questions about Reed and my relationship. He started off by saying how he had never seen a love as deep between two heterosexual women. It was evident every time Reed was at the brink of death because when he would say, "Stay for Lita," it made her pull through every time. When she would talk about the sacrifices I made for her and how she felt safe and secure in my arms when struggling or in pain, her eyes would light up. He knew of our importance to each other but couldn't understand how I was able to put the time I did into Reed and take care of my family. I explained to him how understanding and supportive my husband had been and how we both wanted Reed to have someone in her life during her last days.

That conversation led to many others. Nurse Ryan started texting me when he wanted to give a whole dialogue. One night, Nurse Ryan shared with me that Reed was in extreme pain, and he couldn't hold back his tears. Reed saw that he was crying and took her thumb and wiped the tears from his eyes. At that moment, he looked at her not as his patient but as a mother. Before then, Nurse Ryan had never compared anyone to his mother. He felt that no one could even come close to the type of relationship they had, but what he felt at that moment was both surprising and emotional. Through Reed's wisdom and her spirit to care for others beyond herself, she had truly captured his heart. I thought how beautiful that was and asked if he would consider sharing that with her. He let me know he would when the time was right.

Seeing the miracles of God made Nurse Ryan become more curious to know him. He started asking Reed questions, and Reed would give him the basics on how to pray and explained to him what it meant to be saved. The more time they spent together, the more he inquired and the closer to salvation he became. His involvement not only allowed him to receive spiritually, but it made him see life on a level he had never experienced before. He learned to trust someone else to do his job, even though he was the expert, and no matter what the doctor said, before making any decisions, he would always consult with me. This kept me on my face before God and as he was growing in the Lord, so was I.

One evening when I got home from church, I received an e-mail from Nurse Ryan. Earlier that day, Reed was admitted to the hospital because she was raped in her home. I didn't know how to respond. While trying to process what I just read, I get a phone call from Reed. Trying to sound normal when I answered the phone, I picked up and in a soft tone said, "Hello."

Reed came right out and said, "I just got raped."

I remained silent. I wasn't sure if I should ask questions or just sit on the phone and let her talk, but when I did decide to say something, the first thing that came out of my mouth was, "What happened?" and as she began to try and articulate the traumatic experience, I felt anger rising in me. Knowing that this wasn't the right time, I suppressed what I was feeling and listened as she tried to explain.

Reed started by saying that the evening was no different than any other evening. She checked on her live-in client, then went into the living room to make sure that the doors were locked before heading to the bathroom. When she came out, she was immediately hit in the head with the butt of a gun and dragged into her bedroom, which was right across from the bathroom. When Reed fully came to, there were two white males standing over her. One was holding a gun to her head with his hand over her mouth while the other was holding a knife to her neck, and they were in the process of raping her, one at a time, repeatedly.

The men started to degrade her through name-calling in adjunction to admiring how tight she was. They told her what they were going to do to her before they did it, and when they felt they had enough of the front position, they flipped her over to continue the abuse from the back. Reed was bleeding badly, and the more she cried in pain and in fear, the harder they pounded. After a half an hour into the rape, one of the men left the room while the other continued the abuse. When he was finished, while putting on his pants, he blurted out a few more absurd words and reassured her that they would be back.

Sitting in a pool of blood, Reed began to weep before calling hospice, which they called the police. When they arrived, the officers couldn't believe the scene they had entered. Reed was stripped naked from the waist down and very swollen. The police asked Reed to go to the hospital to take a rape kit test and then returned home. Reed stopped talking and I remained quiet. The silence broke when Reed began to say how when she was growing up, many girls her age were required to sell their bodies, but she was never asked or forced to. She questioned why in her forties would her virginity have to be taken away and in this manner. She couldn't understand how God would allow this to happen to her with everything else that she had to endure. I had no answers because I was feeling the exact same way. My thoughts were to find these men and put them in the hospital, but I knew my anger would not help her in this situation right now, so I did what I felt was best and that was to try and build her back up. The more I began to encourage, the less convinced I became myself. All the confusion, the pain, and the neglect she felt from God, I felt as well, but I had to keep this to myself and find a way to help her. Daily, I would work hard to try and build up her self-esteem, but every time I built her up, the enemy would break her back down. He used this experience to monopolize by constantly saying to her how he sent those men to strip her and will continue to strip her until there's nothing left. That the rape was the only way a man would ever touch her and how she meant nothing to God because he allowed this to happen. At this point, he was winning because Reed was ready to give up, but I prayed. I prayed hard and asked God to give me exactly what she needed. God brought back to my remembrance what Nurse Ryan had said about Reed. That was the answer, so I contacted him and told him now was the time. After hearing how much she meant to him, Reed felt as though she had purpose again, that she was more than just a piece of meat to men, and that she had more to live for. With her spirits now lifted, Nurse Ryan felt it would be a clever idea to have Reed go to a support group. When she went, she wasn't ready to share; however, it did do some good in the sense that she was around other people who was able to relate.

One evening, when Nurse Ryan was supposed to bring Reed to her support group, I received a text from him saying that his wife was in a fatal car accident and he would be staying at the hospital. He told me to let Reed know and he would get back with me later. A few days passed and he texted me and said that while he was at the hospital with his wife and he was having shortness of breath, he got checked out and found that he had pneumonia. He went on to say that he was admitted to the hospital and for me not to worry because he'll be out soon for Reed and me.

Ten days later, it was my birthday and I was so excited because I was given the opportunity to preach at a multicultural fellowship. Before I left the house that afternoon, I did something out of the norm and checked my e-mail. I received an e-mail titled, "Ryan Smith Passing." Afraid to open it, I stepped away from the computer and told God, "Please don't let this be happening," but sure enough when I clicked on it, it was a letter from Nurse Ryan's aunt, stating that he had passed away earlier that day from pneumonia. I was frozen with disbelief. This was a man that not only took excellent care of Reed but, within three months' time, developed a friendship of complete trust, influenced my prayer life, and made me believe more in myself. I was devastated. I always thanked him for what he did for Reed but regretted not thanking him for the impact he had in my life. After receiving this news, I was afraid to tell Reed in fear of how she would react, but when I told her, she mourned silently. At this point, we both knew the team we built was now gone, and it was going to take some time for us both to adjust, but I thank God that in his last days, he got to know Christ and his life was fulfilled.

After the passing of Nurse Ryan, his best friend, Nurse Kent, visited Reed at the hospital and told her that he wanted to be her new primary nurse. Nurse Ryan had always raved about this extraordinary patient of his, so Nurse Kent felt it would only be right to carry on in his stead. Nurse Kent was a tall light-skinned pretty boy who was invested in his possessions. Like Nurse Ryan, he served in the marines for four years before working in the hospice division at the hospital. Nurse Kent was a supervisor who lived in a beautiful home with his wife and three children and had no problem telling anyone of his salary or the type of car he drove. For some, he was considered living the American dream, and that was something he worked hard to sustain.

Shortly after visiting Reed, Nurse Kent got in contact with me. I was relieved to know that we had a replacement as quickly as we did. I felt that with him being so close to Nurse Ryan that things would run just as smoothly as before, but what I failed to realize was that even though they were best friends, they still were two totally different people who did things differently. Nurse Kent started off trying to do as Nurse Ryan would have done, and I held him to the standard that Nurse Ryan set, so with us both in error, we always bumped heads and lacked the communication needed to properly care for Reed. After seeing how this wasn't working, we got together through text to acknowledge our concerns, expectations, and differences and came up with some type of compromise for the sake of Reed.

After a few adjustments, we were on the same page, and that's when Nurse Kent decided to get personal. I believe he was more skeptical than anything and wanted to know more about these two women who had impacted his friend's life, but when he would ask questions, I responded with the bare minimum. After a while, he got the hint and decided that he would open about his personal life in hopes that I would return the favor. He started by sharing with me how Nurse Ryan always wanted to have children but his wife didn't, so to make peace in the home, Nurse Ryan avoided the subject altogether, although Nurse Kent saw that the desire was still there. Already having three children of his own, Nurse Kent and his wife found out that they were going to have a baby boy added to their family. They asked Nurse Ryan if he would consider being the godfather and having the baby named after him. After being asked, Nurse Ryan was so ecstatic that he went out and started buying diapers, clothes, and formula for the baby. He started to tell anyone who would listen how spoiled his godson was going to be. Then Nurse Kent expressed that with all of the preparation Nurse Ryan did, he would never have the chance to see his godson. He started asking me questions about God, and the conversation he thought was intended to get information on Reed and I became a setup for God to begin revealing himself.

Just a few months after Nurse Ryan's passing, Nurse Kent introduced his son into the world. It was bittersweet because his best friend wasn't there, plus his newborn became terminally ill just days after his birth. Being a devout Catholic, Nurse Kent felt he needed more than what he could offer for his son to survive, so the first thing he did was ask Reed if she would go to the hospital to pray for his son and Reed gladly accepted. When she arrived, she went straight onto the room, acknowledged Nurse Kent, and immediately began praying for the son. While she was praying, Nurse Kent fell to his knees and joined her in the prayer. After Reed finished, she left the hospital room while Nurse Kent remained on his knees.

Two days after Reed's visit, she got extremely ill. I received a text from Nurse Kent explaining to me what happened. Still shocked at what he saw, it took him awhile to even begin to explain. He started off by saying that he went over to Reed's house to check on her. When he arrived, she looked as if she was sleeping, but after he called her name a few times and noticed there was absolutely no movement, he took her vitals and couldn't hear a heartbeat. After doing everything he could to revive her, she still didn't respond and he had to call it. His next challenge was trying to find a way to tell me that she was gone. He paced back and forth in the living room as he waited for the morgue to come and get her body. He decided that once they picked up the body, he would then give me that dreadful call. The people from the morgue arrived, and by this time, the stiffness of death had already set in. They got the report, put the toe tag on her, zipped her up in the bag, and started to take her out on the gurney. On their way out, something started to happen. They could hear a small whimper under the zipped bag. At first, they all ignored it, but then the whimper was followed by subtle movements. They opened the bag and saw one tear streaming down Reed's face. Nurse Kent immediately took her vitals and discovered that she had a faint heartbeat, so they rushed her to the hospital. After he told me, all I could do was just look up and say, "Thank you, Jesus." I knew at that movement that the experience was designed especially for him.

After seeing what he witnessed to be a miracle, Nurse Kent became more intrigued. He became so interested to know more about God that Reed began to do Bible study with him twice a week, and after a couple of weeks into it, Nurse Kent told Reed that he wanted to be baptized, so Reed took him outside to the pool area at her apartment complex and baptized him in Jesus's Name. When he came up from the water, he began speaking in tongues as Reed watched the birth of this new soul.

I was so happy to hear that he had received the Holy Ghost. He shared with me the things Reed taught him in Bible study, and he also shared his admiration and attraction he had developed toward her. He knew nothing would become of it because not only was it against work policy but he was a happily married man, and he felt comfortable enough to express this to me. I thought I'll take advantage of this information, and I asked him if he could just let Reed know that he admired her. My reasoning behind it was that this would be something that would lift her self-esteem, which she was still battling with, so to have this handsome man tell her that he admired her would definitely be flattering.

The very next day, Nurse Kent told Reed completely how he felt about her. Little did I know, Reed felt the exact same way. With them both being googly eyed for each other, the conversation ended with Nurse Kent saying, "You know that nothing could become of this," and although Reed knew and understood that, emotionally, she was not ready to accept it.

A few months went by, and although things were a bit uncomfortable between Reed and Nurse Kent, they were still able to keep that patient/client relationship. One evening as Reed was getting ready for bed, she received a text from who she thought was Nurse Kent, but it was from his wife. She stated that Nurse Kent was at the hospital and asked if Reed would pray for him. Reed said that she would, and as soon as the conversation ended, Reed started to pray. She then called me to tell me what had just happened. I told her that I would be praying as well and then we said good night.

I prayed diligently for Nurse Kent two nights in a row, and God kept revealing to me the cause of his illness, but because it seemed so far-fetched, I chose to ignore it. It kept bothering my spirit, however, so I asked Reed the next time she heard from Nurse Kent if she could ask him to contact me, and she said she would. Not long after my conversation with Reed, Nurse Kent made contact, and the first thing that he told me was that while he was in the hospital, his newborn baby had passed away and his wife got him cremated before he had the chance to say goodbye. He then asked me, "Why would God allow this to happen?"

I tried to answer him the best way I could by using less Bible and more comfort because that was what he needed at the time. As I began to comfort him, the questions I wanted to ask him about his illness took a back seat, and it was days past before I could contact him again.

When we made contact, Nurse Kent was feeling much better than before. He told me that he was taking some time off to go on vacation with his family and he would be back within a week, but because he wasn't going to take his work phone, Nurse Kent instructed me to have Reed call him on his personal phone if needed. I agreed and he left for vacation. While he was away, God brought back what he told me during those two days of prayer. Even though I didn't want to bother Nurse Kent, I knew I had to give him this information, so I told Reed to contact him and tell him to be careful what he eats or drink around his wife because she was poisoning him. Reed didn't question what was said, she just responded with an okay and made contact immediately. After Reed gave the message, he said that he had the same feeling after noticing a change in his wife's behavior toward him and that he would be more careful around her. I felt somewhat relieved because I told him what thus saith the Lord and discovered that it was confirmation. While he was away, Reed had a severe episode, which made her become hospitalized. I didn't want to interrupt Nurse Kent's vacation any further so I didn't say anything to him, but he happened to be checking in with his job and found out that Reed was admitted. Without notice, Nurse Kent immediately flew back to see what was going on. When he arrived, he contacted me and said he would only be there for a few days before he had to go back. That was the extent to our conversation; however, he asked me a question that caught my attention. He wanted to know what was mine and Nurse Ryan's conversation before he passed. I told him it wasn't much because he was being admitted to the hospital. He responded and ended the conversation by saying, "I love my boy, but I don't want to end up dead like him."

It's ironic that those were his last words to me because two days later, his job called Reed and told her that Nurse Kent was dead. No words could describe that moment for both Reed and me. He had so much more to live for and things were looking better for him, but before his life ended, he got to know God as his personal savior and is now able to see God in peace. The love he saw his best friend had for others drew him to the love of God, and that's what matters most.

# THE BATTLES CONTINUES

A few weeks after Nurse Kent passed, we had another replacement, a young nurse named Reggie. Nurse Reggie took over in curiosity. He wanted to know more about this woman he heard so much about throughout the hospital. When Nurse Reggie first came to introduce himself to Reed as her new nurse, he walked in her room as if he owned the place. He had deep dimples, was always well dressed, and wore the most flattering cologne that not only grabbed people's attention but gave him an air of cockiness. Although he was the youngest of the nurses, he had a deep rich voice that when heard was as addictive as a cup of Folger's roasted coffee. Although he had that going for him, it didn't impress Reed one bit. Being very skeptical of Nurse Reggie and not wanting to become as attached as she did with the others, she kept him at arm's length and had very little to say.

Reed challenged Nurse Reggie every way possible. Not only because of his age, but to see if he could handle being her nurse. No matter what was done to him, Nurse Reggie never backed away from a challenge and proved to Reed that he was equipped to handle the job. One night, Nurse Reggie shared with Reed that he had a passion to cook. When he offered to cook for her, that arm's length between them began to slowly close. He had now piqued Reed's interest, but she wouldn't be impressed until she tasted his cooking. When Nurse Reggie began cooking, he had Reed's place smelling like a restaurant. He made steak, enchiladas, and whatever else she wanted. Reed became happier that she had a personal chef and a personal nurse, and once she allowed herself to open, it was easy for all of us to fit in our proper places.

After being introduced to Nurse Reggie, we hit it off immediately. He had professional tendencies, but unlike the other nurses, his approach was very engaging. When he became Reed's nurse, the hospital had already made changes to their nurse's handbook on its policies after finding out that Nurse Ryan had been in communication with me. From that point on, all nurses' work phones were tapped, and they were limited to its usage. Knowing what was done before, Nurse Reggie would text me on Reed's phone to give his reports, before graduating to e-mails and a personal cell phone to further communicate.

After Nurse Ryan's death, Reed and I had a break in battling with the enemy. He would show up here and there but wasn't as prominent as he was when Nurse Ryan was alive. I guess he figured that his vacation from us was now over because as soon as Nurse Reggie came into the picture, so did he. It was hard explaining to the nurses what was happening anytime Reed and I were in battle while they were present. Most of the time, I would ask them to go into the living room, and if I needed their assistance, I would text them. This night, I was talking on the phone with Reed. Nurse Reggie was there, and everything seemed to be going well. Suddenly, Reed screamed in pain, and when I asked her what happened, there was complete silence. Nurse Reggie took the phone and texted me what he saw. I instructed him to go into the living room and just check on her periodically. Not knowing that he never left the room, I knew this was a spiritual battle and began to fight. After the victorious outcome, Nurse Reggie immediately texted me and told me something that flesh and blood could not reveal. I was in total shock. Every time I would bring up God or the church, he would tell me that he didn't want to hear about it and that would be the end of the conversation. So when I asked him how he got that revelation, he avoided my question and proceeded with his nurse duties.

The very next day, I received an e-mail from Nurse Reggie. In the e-mail, he began explaining to me the reason for his attitude toward God and the church. His dad was a pastor of one of the biggest Apostolic churches in Southern California. He served close with his dad in ministry, hoping to one day follow in his footsteps. As one of their community outreach services, Nurse Reggie and his dad would deliver groceries to the homes of single parents once a week. One night, Nurse Reggie went to the van to get more groceries as his dad began carrying a bag of groceries around the corner to the woman's doorsteps. Before he could ring the doorbell, a man came out of the bushes and stabbed him over sixteen times. By the time Nurse Reggie got to him, the man was gone, and Nurse Reggie was left holding his dad in his arms as he watched him die. Shortly after the passing of his father, his mother also died of what they believe was a broken heart. Nurse Reggie continued by saying that while in ministry, he was constantly abused by the hands of leaders whom they fellowshipped with, but he never said anything in fear that he wouldn't be believed. After reading the e-mail, I just sat there in awe. As unfortunate as it was, it made so much sense as to why he understood the spiritual battles and the exposure of his spiritual giftings. I thought of the scripture in the Bible that says, "All gifts come without repentance." Despite his current state, there was no denying the power of God in his life.

After that confession, Nurse Reggie was put in positions where he had to use what God had given him. His desire to protect Reed and support me became the fuel that pushed him past his boundaries. Within no time, we became partners in battling the enemy. Things I couldn't see or understand, he had the knowledge of, which gave me insight on the enemy's tactics before he would strike. At some point, my tactics against the enemy became predictable, and although I didn't pay too much attention to it, through the spirit, Nurse Reggie did and he would tell me when I needed to change it up. This made the enemy confused and even more vengeful, but it helped and gave us the advantage.

One night while Nurse Reggie was on duty, God began dealing with him on forgiveness and he brought the subject up to Reed. Not too long into their discussion did God reveal to her what Nurse Reggie had went through growing up in the church. Once she began to speak it outwardly to him, a deliverance service started right there in the room and he got reclaimed. The enemy lost again and wasn't too happy to say the least. Not only was a soul snatched from hell, but Nurse Reggie became a vital part of the warfare against him. Nurse Reggie, Reed, and I came from the same spiritual background, so our ways of doing and understanding things were similar, which made the partnership easier but fueled the enemy that much more to try and tear us apart.

During spiritual battles, the enemy would leave me messages to try to intimidate me. One time, he left a message, saying, "I am pulling them both down before they get started. I am going to afflict her and strip him. He's open, she's open. I already took his money, and I'm stirring up conflict in his family. I'm taking back what belongs to me. You can't fight for both, you must choose. They are about to turn on you. They are despondent, angry, and poor. It has already begun."

Immediately after I received the message, Reed called me screaming in pain as Nurse Reggie texted me, saying that he was driving and had to pull over because his head felt like it was about to explode. The enemy then said to me again, "You can't save them both, you have to choose."

With no fear, I laid flat on my face and began calling out both their names before God. Can't no devil in hell tell me who I can and cannot save. This was one of my most intense two minutes battles of my life because it was over shortly after it started. The hand of the enemy had to be released, and when things were back to normal, I went on telling them both what had just occurred.

That battle began many physical battles for Nurse Reggie, which occurred one after the other. He got into a car accident and injured his head, then he was jumped which did more damage to his head, followed by poisoning and rape. Because of all the trauma done to his head, he lay in a coma for months. With all of what was happening to Nurse Reggie, he still helped Reed and me as much as he could during the spirituals battles. He would relay messages from his hospital bed through family members, and it would be very useful in guiding and supporting us before, during, and after the battles. While in the hospital, Nurse Reggie told me to take a break from battle for a week and he would take care of Reed. I was unsure because I was always there to battle for and with her, and quite frankly, I didn't trust anyone else, but because I was exhausted during this time, I went ahead and let him take charge. One day, during that week, I received an instant message from pastors in Africa stating that Nurse Reggie organized a week shut in with numerous churches to fast and pray on Reed's behalf. They went on encouraging me to continue to fight for the woman of God and left me with some suggestions for things to come. I was impressed to say the least. I didn't know Nurse Reggie was going to gather people from an entire continent to pray on Reed's behalf, but he did and at the end of it all my job was to just love on her until she was restored. Shortly after the shut in, Nurse Reggie became less and less in the picture because of his illnesses. His uncle had him go down to Southern California where he would be close to family and received hospital care in hopes of him going back to Sacramento, well and ready to work.

One month passed, then two, then three, and I hadn't heard from Nurse Reggie. Usually when I didn't hear directly from him, his uncle or cousin would get in contact with me to let me know what was going on. My birthday came around, and I didn't receive a text from Nurse Reggie, nor did any of his relatives contact me. No matter what state Nurse Reggie would be in, when my birthday came around, he would always contact me. I knew something was wrong, but I tried to dismiss my worries with the excuse of maybe he was unable to find a way to communicate and he will contact me soon. December came and I still hadn't heard from him, but instead, I received a general e-mail from his cousin asking how I was doing. I responded by asking had he heard from his cousin, and that's when he told me. Nurse Reggie had passed away in the hospital July of 2013. I was both in shock and devastated. I had lost not only my spiritual partner but my friend. We laughed together, cried together, prayed together, and had several disagreements, but through it all, we covered each other, and as in any good relationship, it was hard to let go. I thank God for the time Nurse Reggie and I shared and the soul that was once lost, was now reclaimed, and brought back to God.

During the times when Nurse Reggie was sick, he brought in another nurse who I referred to as Doc. Doc was a white male, over seven feet tall, who had the face of a model. He cared about his patients, but unlike the other nurses, he didn't show much emotion. Doc's first interaction with me was straight business. In giving his report, he would include the time of each activity, military style. I had to think back to when I was in high school's JROTC so I could equate military time with standard time because he would throw it out there like it was a part of everyone's daily vocabulary. After making jokes about it to him, he opened up and we were able to begin working together. With each nurse, it was a partnership. They took care of the natural and I took care of the spiritual, and we both took care of the needs of Reed. Even though Doc's and my personalities were compatible, it took some time for us to get accustomed to how we each functioned. Doc's method was straight to the letter, and mine was spirit led, so there were many discrepancies between us in dealing with Reed. At times, Nurse Reggie had to be the mediator to get us both to see each other's side, and although we bumped heads trying, we eventually found a method that worked for the both of us.

Soon Doc found himself out of his comfort zone by also going above and beyond for Reed. He was the one nurse who received the most write-ups for violating policy, and it became so often that it was like a fix-it ticket; he glanced at it and then threw it aside. As passionate about his job as he was, it didn't interfere with spending time with his family. Doc had a wife and four beautiful children whom he adored, and he would often schedule trips on the weekend for them to get away to do some kayaking. He was a hands-on dad who did hair, took the kids to school, and helped with homework. Doc's life was well balanced, and although he was content with what he had, he was about to be introduced to something he would have never felt he needed, and that was a relationship with God.

Reed was always in and out of the hospital, but this time, it had got to the point where she was put on life support. It wasn't even a few days before the hospital's administration was making plans to take her off. Doc and Reggie fought hard to keep her on for a couple more days and told me the severity of the situation. To them, my reaction was as if I wasn't taking the situation seriously, but I was waiting on God for guidance. Before the allotted time they gave Reed to expired, I told Doc to take Reed off the life support. He responded as if I was crazy and reiterated the severity of the situation. I told him I understood, but she needed to be taken off. He said, "You do know once we take her off, she's gone right?"

I said, "Take her off, if it's ever a time to trust God, now is the time."

They all thought I had lost my mind. Doc told Nurse Reggie of my decision and said he would not have any part of it, so he left the hospital right before they took Reed off. Two hours after he left, they called him back and told him after she had been off the support for over an hour, they were about to take her down to the morgue and heard a whimper and saw signs of life. Doc couldn't believe it. According to all the signs, there was no way she was supposed to live. This miracle allowed all to witness the power of God and to let him know that God is real.

That was an experience that made Doc spiritually receptive. God started using him in ways he was unaware. In this battle of natural and spiritual, each nurse had their place, and Doc was used as an anchor to stabilize and keep everything in place. Sometimes, the battles would be so intense that afterward, I would be all over the place emotionally. Doc would send me an e-mail or text just to encourage me in a calm manner that only he could give and that would put me back in focus. He never realized that it was exactly what was needed, but it was becoming evident that God placed him in my life for that very purpose.

One evening, Doc sent me a message, asking how does Reed do it. I asked him to clarify what he meant, and he said with all that she endures, how could she still be strong enough to continue to fight another day. I told him it was because of the strength she regains by having a relationship with God. Doc was very intrigued and he wanted to know more about God. The very next day, he went to Reed's house and sat at her feet and began to glean everything he could to learn about God. Doc was very intelligent, so he comprehended quickly and was open enough to receive what God had for him. One night, Reed was in the hospital, and Doc went up there to take her home. While she was being discharged, the Holy Spirit filled the room where they were in, and Doc began to speak in other tongues. He was so full that instead of him waiting for the wheelchair that was sent for Reed, he carried her to the car himself, and as he walked down the hallways, he was still speaking in other tongues. Soon thereafter, Reed referred him to a church so he could get baptized. Being that he was over seven feet tall, it was hard for them to find some clothes that fit him. They baptized him in an outfit that looked like the wardrobe of Incredible Hulk, but despite how Doc looked, he was excited about his spiritual experiences.

As his spiritual life was increasing, his personal life began to go haywire. One of his sons got ill and the passed away; shortly afterward, his brother and father passed away almost simultaneously, and his marriage as he knew it was over. His entire world crashed down within a matter of a few years. I wanted so much to be there for him in person, to hold him and tell him that everything would be okay. My Doc, who was once an anchor for me, now needed that in return. Despite our distance, I tried everything I could to support him during this time of his life, but in his process, he lost his desire for many things, which included his newfound faith. I respected the state that he was in and was careful of what I said, but I could sense that he was sinking fast and I knew if God didn't intervene soon that he would either hurt someone else or be hurt. He flew to Chicago to get away for a few days, and while he was out there, he contacted me to let me know where he was. His e-mail sounded as though he wasn't in his right mind, so I e-mailed him back and told him whatever he was thinking about doing, to stop for a minute, take out a picture of his children, and look at them closely. I asked him whatever he wanted to do was it worth hurting his children and changing their lives forever. He broke down and repented and told me, "No, it wasn't," and left Chicago the very next morning

For several months, I heard little from Doc. I knew he was trying to get his life in order so I continued to cover him and his family in prayer. It wasn't until I received an e-mail from him that put me at total ease. He wrote, "I was thinking about you today and thanking

God for allowing me to have you in my life. I started reading my Bible again, and God was showing me that I need a relationship with him. I called Ms. Reed and was telling her that I didn't know how to handle everything that was going on in my life and how I felt as though I didn't have any direction. She really helped me by telling me to turn it over to God and ask him for direction and to have faith in believing that he will work it out. I must use my faith in trusting God with what I am facing and know that whatever I face, he can handle it. I'm so glad she was there to help me."

Shortly after that e-mail, Doc moved him and his children out of state to take care of his mother. The last time I received an e-mail from him was in 2012, stating that he was starting his life over, and once he gets settled, I'll hear back from him. I never heard back from him again. Once again, Reed and I lost a great man, but as with those before him, he was introduced to God and received salvation, so now wherever life takes him, God is right there.

# Just the Two of Us

At this point in our lives, to have a permanent nurse was no longer a luxury. There were those who came afterward for a short season, some even received Christ in the process, but then they were all swept away as leaves fallen from a tree. Nurse Shelly, an older lady who had been in this field for a long time, she was the eyes and ears for both Reed and I while Reed was in the hospital. She kept me updated and allowed me to have direct contact with her.

Nurse Kate was another nurse who looked out for Reed. Even when she wasn't on duty, she would go to the hospital to check on Reed. Nurse Kate and I developed a good relationship, and it was so easy to work with her. She was a caring and affectionate person, which showed in everything she did.

Despite protocol, the supervisor would even contact me to give updates about Reed. She was described by her employees as cold and heartless. As I interacted with her more, God began to reveal her past to me and the hurt she carried for many years. After ministering to her, not only did she get reclaimed, but she apologized to her entire staff for her behavior and asked each of them individually for forgiveness. That was a momentous moment not only for her but for those she supervised.

Nurse Dean was Reed's last assigned nurse. He was a white male who was passionate about his job. Although each nurse had their personal relationships with Reed and I, Nurse Dean was the only one who kept it strictly professional with Reed. He was emotionally invested with what she was going through, but he never allowed her to see it. As with almost every nurse, he faced some dark times in his life as well. He had to deal with one of his children becoming sick and infidelity in his marriage, but through it all, Nurse Dean experienced the power of God and although he shockingly passed away as well, the prodigy of his work remains. With them no longer in our lives and Reed living past her expected time, more physical things became apparent. Reed experienced the drowning of her organs by blood, fluids being backed up, sepsis had gotten into her bloodstream, occasional blindness, slow speech, massive heart attacks, strokes, the rotting of her skin, confusion, loss of time, portions of her brain ceasing to function, and countless points of deaths. With all this being less than a five-year span, through prayer, love, and the strength to continue the fight, Reed had conquered it all.

It amazed me to see the effect prayer had as often as I did. By this time, I felt like a miniature pro when it came to praying and battling for Reed, but every time I thought I had it in the bag, God would always allow me to experience another level. My prayers became the shield needed to block the devices of the enemy and restore Reed through my love and support. It was said many times how she shouldn't have been able to reason, walk, talk, or comprehend the way a normal functioning person did, but thanks be to God and the fight in Reed that she remained capable of using the functions of her body.

Reed remained on hospice for four years before they told her that there was nothing more they could do and suggested that she go into a nursing home. This was Reed's biggest fear. Even with her ailments, she was quite independent, and living in a nursing home would strip her of that. We had no other option but to find alternatives. Hospice suggested for Reed to be transferred to a hospital where they were experienced in complex health conditions. After doing extensive resource on the hospital, we agreed that this would be the better option, and soon, Reed became adjusted.

At every weak point in Reed's life, the enemy sought opportunity to attack. I found myself making trips one weekend a month just to take care and go into spiritual battle on Reed's behalf. My first personal encounter with the enemy was one in which a person would have never expected. This weekend that I went up there, Reed was having a tough time physically. No matter what was done there seemed to be no release from her pain and helpless as I felt, I just watched and prayed. It was midnight, and Reed told me that she had to go the bathroom but felt that it wasn't safe for her to go. I told her it would be okay and reassured her that I'll be right by the door the entire time, but she insisted on not going. She then asked if she could lie on my lap, and as she began to lie down, I heard the voice of the enemy shouting, "Get her!"

Her body sprung out of bed and headed straight toward the wall. Without thinking, I grabbed her before she made contact, pulled her to the bed, held her body down with my legs, and put her arms behind her back as I have seen done many times in wrestling. The voice began to get louder and repeatedly screamed, "Get her! Get her!" as I was simultaneously screaming, "In the name of Jesus!"

After what seemed like forever, there was silence. I eased my grip a little, and Reed's body sprung up and ran into the wall and began beating in her head. I immediately tackled her down to the floor and then I heard a small voice call out my name. I noticed that Reed had come to, and I let her go as we sat on the floor at the bottom of the bed. After I caught my breath, I asked her did she know what had just happened. She told me no, not at all, but she did have a message from the Lord. At this point, I was so relieved because I had no idea what was going on and my support group that I would have leaned on was no longer. So I waited in anticipation as God began to speak through Reed, saying, "This is a battle that you must fight. Your angel is tied up elsewhere, but you can do it, I'm with you."

I then looked at her as if something more was going to be said, but nothing more followed and so my next thought was how my angel could be somewhere else and during a time like this. I was baffled, but regardless of how confused I was, the battle did not wait for me to get over my feelings because the second round began almost immediately after I was given those words from God. We ended up on the bed again, in the same wrestling position. After a while God told me that the enemies time was about to expire. Right after God's words to me, the enemy said, "Get her, we don't have that much time left."

The battle went on for another ten minutes and then I heard Reed's voice. The first thing that came out her mouth was, "Lita, why am I between your legs?"

Still wanting to make sure I wouldn't make the same mistake twice, I asked her a few questions and held her in the position I had just a little while longer before releasing her. After letting her go, I began to explain what just happened the best way I knew how and then told her to get some rest. When she finally fell asleep, I watched her the entire night without any more interference from the enemy.

That weekend became one of many occasions where the enemy was consistently present. He became very prominent in Reed's life and was determined that he would take her out by any means necessary. Through our many battles, the enemy and I became very acquainted. He communicated with me through text by influencing Reed's body. It had gotten to the point where I would use what was said to get a better understanding of the enemy's plans. His messages began to read as threats saying things like, "I told you I had her. Give up, let her go, you've already lost. You think you're going to fight for her? She's weak, she has no strength. I need to get rid of you. I'm taking her away from your influence, your prayers. Your biggest fear is about to happen, she will turn against you. I've been waiting a long time for this, but I'm patient, shoot your best shot, it won't work, I have control of her."

He even tried to bargain with me, and when I asked why all this fuss over Reed, he said it was because even though she doesn't look like much and people underestimate her a lot, she is more of a threat to him than those popular pastors and preachers with mega ministries. He was tired of her taking away what belonged to him, and with the type of influence she has over people, he needed someone like that to lead his army. The enemy continued by explaining how Reed's illness and mental state was access for him to block and filter what he desired. He would block the positive reinforcements and filter in his words, ideas, her past, and anything that he thought would break her, as well as cause a wedge between the two of us. The more he talked, the more he exposed himself, and the more I began to understand.

Through the conversations the enemy and I had, I became more spiritually equipped. However, there were some setbacks because there were times where it was hard to distinguish between Satan, the illness, or just Reed's personality. Even though I knew to deal with them separately, it became challenging when sometimes they all seemed to be muddled together. These were the times where God had to personally minister to me, and in doing so, God would tell me how pleased he was of me and always reminded me of his love for Reed and the reason he continued to spare her life was because he committed her unto my hands and it was for me to continue to uphold her until her purpose was fulfilled.

As time went on, the enemy was less present and God had spoken to me and told me that during this time of his absence, this was her season to enjoy life, and that's exactly what we began doing. We started taking trips to Reno, San Francisco, and even dared to go on death-defying rides. For the first time in our relationship, we could experience the pleasure of being outdoors. I was so happy to share a moment like this with Reed, and she was even happier to have these experiences where the pain didn't interfere with her enjoyment. Not only was this a refresher for the relationship, but it had given us a deeper sense of love and admiration for one another.

# No Greater Love

Today in our society, it seems to be one-dimensional when it comes to love, affection, or desire. Sex and lust is just some of the things we limit ourselves to when proclaiming our love for each other. I thought I understood what it meant to love being that I was married for twenty years, but having the experiences I had with Reed, I found out there is more to love than what we could even comprehend.

The Bible speaks of four different types of love, the greater being Agape. The reason this love is esteemed higher than the others is because, first, it demonstrates God's love for us, and unlike the others, it is happy in giving and continues to give even if the person is unresponsive. This was the type of love Reed and I had. It was not what I could get, but what I could give. So many people who came in Reed's life only did so because of her illness, and that's why it was so easy for them to leave when things got hard; however, for us, it wasn't her illness that brought us together, but it was our love for each other. With each experience we had, our love continued to grow. I knew the love we shared was special when God would always remind me during our battles with the enemy that our love was the key and it was because it pulled Reed through every time. No matter how hard the enemy tried, love always won.

Even with all the love we had, it was hard sometimes. There were times where I chose not to express my feelings and concerns to Reed. One reason being how she would receive it. The second being the enemy would use what was said and distort it for his benefit.

Although as a friend I wanted to voice certain things, I had to be wise when knowing what to say or if to say anything at all.

Seven years of operating the way I did with Reed, I started to notice some changes in my marriage. My husband and I sat down to discuss what was going on, and he shared with me that the time I had given to others might have been beneficial for them, but it had caused a wedge between him and I. Some would say that this should have been obvious to me, but it wasn't and I was in total shock. All the time I took away from my home, the time I was accustomed to giving someone else, now needed to be redirected. We decided to seek professional help and so we saw a marriage counselor for six weeks to help us eliminate the distance between us. Even though my love and devotion for Reed had never changed through this process, I knew the dynamics of our relationship must change to save my marriage. Little by little, I began to make changes in my routine, and as subtle as I thought I was being, Reed caught on quick. I never told her the reason for the changes in fear that she would detach herself altogether, but a part of me felt like she already knew. We went from talking on the phone at least three times a day for hours to me not hearing from Reed at all. The changes in our relationship became harder for both of us to adjust to. She felt that I was no longer available for her, and I started to find out what was going on in her life through social media exclusively. So with these changes, it began to cause a wedge between us.

One evening, Reed called me, and the conversation went right into us reminiscing about the things we've experienced together. We hadn't laughed that hard in a while, and despite the separation we created, the love we had built over the years was apparent. Before we got off the phone, Reed said, "Lita, I first want to thank God for blessing me with such a beautiful and wonderful friend. You have impacted my life in so many unmeasurable ways. Down through the years, you have accepted me for who I was without any hidden motives. You restored me and helped me to believe in myself again. I had been used and abused by so many and was always giving and never receiving. It came to a point that all the love I was giving was thrown back into my face. I had been hurt to the point that I didn't trust and was afraid to love, but because of your faith in me and your love in me, you opened my heart to love, my arms to hug, my emotions to trust, and my spirit to give. We have laughed until it hurt and laughed until we could not laugh anymore. We have cried, we have shared our very intimate secrets, our fears, and our insecurities. Our friendship and love has been tested and tried and we have come out as pure gold. You have grown so much spiritually and is such a powerful woman of God. You have been instilled with the word of wisdom and word of knowledge. You have prophesied into the lives of the people of God, and you have spoken and proph-esied life into me. I will be forever grateful. My love for you became deeper and deeper, to the point that if I didn't hear your voice, my day was not complete until I talked with you. When we were together, I felt safe and knew that no matter what was going on, I could trust you with my life. When you hold me, I feel the love that a baby feels when they're in their momma's arms, safe, secure, protected, loved, and no matter what was hurting, no matter how extreme the pain, I knew being in your arms may not take away the hurt or pain, but made it easier to bear. So from the bottom of my heart, I thank you for your embrace of love, but now, I feel it's time for me to go. I must leave so that you can live. Lita, I want you to live and not have to worry about me any longer. I pray the peace of God over you, that he would comfort you, and that you will know you are not alone I am here with you, though we're far apart, you're always in my heart."

The entire time tears were rolling down my face, but I never gave her any inkling that I was crying because if this was going to be our last memory, I wanted it to be special. I asked her if this was something she really wanted to do, and she said, "Yes, it's time."

Soon, the death rattle became apparent. I remembered past conversations with the nurses explaining to me that if I ever heard a rattle in Reed's voice, it meant that she was close to death, so I went with my first instinct and started singing Michael Jackson's "You Are Not Alone." I would sing this song to Reed during the times when she was experiencing excruciating pain, and it would relax her to the point where she would fall asleep. As I began to sing, the rattling started to dissipate, and all I heard was Reed struggling to take her last few breaths and then it went completely silent. I called out her name, and with no answer, I held the phone to my heart and wept.

*"Greater love has no one than this: to lay down*
*one's life for one's friends." (John 5:13)*

# Epilogue

Over fifteen years since we met and Reed is still alive. She continues to reside in Sacramento, California, where God has anointed her as pastor, and not only does she support and assist other pastors but she continues to travel and preach the word of God. There were many times throughout our journey together where we thought Reed's time had come to an end. Reed had never wanted to die, but her experiences between life and death, her visitation to heaven witnessing loved ones, and her being in the presence of Jesus Christ, lessen her desire to stay. Reed has had more experiences than anyone could imagine, and with the thorn she continues to bear, she will continue to walk this walk of faith until her purpose is complete.

As far as people coming in and out of her life and the physical and emotional struggles she had to deal with, it hasn't changed. The one remarkable thing that has changed in Reed's life is that she now knows her worth. It is a great disadvantage when someone doesn't know their worth because when they began to internalize what other people think or say about them, they then act or react accordingly, and during our battles with the enemy, he knew what to use for his advantage. It wasn't until this one evening were Reed and I were in spiritual battle, and as we were battling, God began to show Reed in the spiritual realm everything that the enemy was doing and why he was so threatened by her. Nothing could give Reed the revelation of herself as this had done, and at that very moment, she took back all power that the enemy held over her for all those years.

As for me, I am doing well. My husband and I have started a ministry, and our marriage continues to flourish. I am so grateful to have a husband who, despite what was taken from him, never stopped me or discouraged me in any way from being myself, fulfilling my purpose, my dreams, and my desires. I also went back to school and received my Associate of Art degree in Music at DVC and I am currently at Cal State East Bay to pursuit my bachelor of art degree in hope of one day becoming a teacher. To this day, the loss of so many of my loved ones still affects me. It's sad to say that most of my meaningful relationships were through text or over the phone, but despite the frustration on both ends because of the limitations, we all still came out to be a better version of ourselves. Who I started as, I am no longer, for I have blossomed into someone that even those I grew up with can't even recognize. I have seen my shortcomings, my strength, and I will continue to enhance myself not only for my well-being but for the benefit of others.

Reed and I are still friends to this day, but the dynamics of our relationship has changed. My need in this friendship became one in which she couldn't understand. I knew with her condition, the constant battles, and a relationship where it was phone based most of the time, it would create limitations, but those immediate needs you would find in any relationship just got lost. Those who were engrafted into our relationship seemed to take a small piece of it when they left, resulting in a hole which was hard to fill. I began to redirect my focus and invest more so in my family, ministry, and school. However, with our separate paths, we will always have each other's back. We've been through everything imaginable, and the fact that God had put us together, nothing can tear us apart. From our friendship came a love that needed to be seen not only for Reed and myself but for those we encountered. A friendship that seemed complex created a bond that even had the enemy baffled and salvation to all those who were willing to accept it.

I've learned that no matter what you face in life, whether it be sickness, neglect, abuse, poverty, etc., having the love and support of a person could make it that much easier for you while going through it. After all that Reed and I had faced together, we are better people because of it. When Reed's purpose is fulfilled and God calls her home, she would not have only left behind her legacy, but the notion that no matter what you face in life (with God by your side) you can come out as pure gold.

# About the Author

Charlita Houston is native to Cleveland, Ohio, but currently lives in California. She is a songwriter, recording artist, and is in the process of retaining her BA degree in music at Cal State University East Bay. Charlita is a wife to a pastor, a mother to three daughters, and a spiritual advisor to many.